PRINCEWILL LAGANG

Dating Deliberately: A Christian's Guide to Relationships

First published by PRINCEWILL LAGANG 2023

Copyright © 2023 by Princewill Lagang

All rights reserved. No part of this publication may be reproduced, stored or transmitted in any form or by any means, electronic, mechanical, photocopying, recording, scanning, or otherwise without written permission from the publisher. It is illegal to copy this book, post it to a website, or distribute it by any other means without permission.

Princewill Lagang asserts the moral right to be identified as the author of this work.

First edition

This book was professionally typeset on Reedsy. Find out more at reedsy.com

Contents

1	The Foundation of Purpose	1
2	Setting the Right Priorities	4
3	Finding the Right Partner	7
4	Nurturing a Purposeful Connection	10
5	Navigating Challenges with Faith and Resilience	13
6	The Beauty of Commitment	16
7	Embracing the Journey with Faith and Purpose	19
8	Conclusion - Embracing God's Plan for Love	22
9	Resources and Recommendations	25
10	A Lifelong Journey	29
11	A Community of Love	32
12	A Continuing Journey	35

1

The Foundation of Purpose

In the quiet corners of a bustling coffee shop, where the aroma of freshly brewed coffee lingered in the air, Sarah sat across from her best friend, Mark. They had been friends for years, sharing countless moments of laughter and support through life's ups and downs. Today, however, the atmosphere was different. Mark leaned in and asked a question that had been on his mind for quite some time.

"Sarah, I've been thinking about something lately, and I wanted to talk to you about it," Mark said with a hint of hesitation.

Sarah, intrigued, took a sip of her cappuccino and replied, "Sure, Mark, what's on your mind?"

"I've been dating for a while now, and it just feels like I'm going from one relationship to the next without any real purpose or direction. I see so many of my friends doing the same thing, and I can't help but wonder if there's a better way, especially for someone with our faith. I mean, we believe in something deeper, right?"

Sarah nodded in agreement, her eyes reflecting Mark's concern. She understood exactly what he meant, and she'd felt the same way at different points in her own dating journey. It was a question that had troubled her heart too.

"Mark, you're not alone in feeling that way. It's something that many Christians grapple with. We believe in building our lives on a foundation of faith, so it makes sense that our approach to relationships should be different," she replied.

As the conversation between Sarah and Mark unfolded, they began to explore the concept of dating deliberately. Their discussion led them to a realization that their faith wasn't just something they practiced on Sundays, but a guiding principle that should permeate every aspect of their lives, including their dating experiences.

In this chapter, we'll delve into the foundation of purpose and intentionality in dating for Christians. Dating deliberately is about finding a relationship that aligns with your faith, values, and long-term goals. It's about understanding that dating is not merely a social pastime but a purposeful journey. As Christians, we are called to live our lives in accordance with our beliefs, and our approach to dating should be no different.

In the pages that follow, we will explore the core principles of dating deliberately, drawing upon biblical wisdom, personal anecdotes, and expert advice to create a comprehensive guide for Christians seeking to navigate the complex world of modern relationships. This book will provide you with the tools and insights you need to date with intention, integrity, and a deep commitment to your faith.

So, if you've ever questioned whether there's a better way to approach dating as a Christian, this chapter is the first step on a transformative journey. Let's explore what it truly means to date deliberately and how to build a strong foundation for your future relationships, all while honoring your faith and the unique path God has set before you.

2

Setting the Right Priorities

As Sarah and Mark continued their conversation about dating deliberately, their shared sense of purpose began to solidify. They knew that to navigate the world of relationships as Christians, setting the right priorities was crucial. In this chapter, we will delve into the foundational principles of establishing priorities in dating, which is the first step toward dating deliberately.

Section 1: The Priority of Faith

In the dimly lit corner of the coffee shop, Mark leaned in, a question still on his mind. "Sarah, I can't help but wonder, should faith be the top priority in our relationships?"

Sarah nodded thoughtfully. "Absolutely, Mark. Faith should be at the core of our priorities in dating. It's the foundation upon which we build our lives as Christians. The Bible teaches us not to be unequally yoked with unbelievers, and this is essential in a romantic relationship. Shared faith provides a deep spiritual connection and common values that are critical for a healthy and lasting relationship."

Section 2: Defining Your Values

A few weeks later, Sarah and Mark were still exploring the concept of priorities in dating, and they decided to meet at the same coffee shop. They both had lists in hand, which they had compiled separately. Sarah spoke first, "Mark, it's important to define our values, those characteristics and attributes that truly matter to us in a partner."

Mark agreed, "I think so too, Sarah. By understanding our values, we can better assess potential partners and determine whether they align with what we hold dear. It's not about creating a perfect checklist, but rather recognizing what's essential for a fulfilling relationship."

Section 3: Long-Term Goals

In their conversation, Sarah brought up another significant point. "Mark, setting priorities also means looking at the long-term. What are your goals, and do they align with your partner's goals? It's essential to discuss and understand where you both see yourselves in the future. Your relationship should be a stepping stone toward your shared goals and aspirations."

Mark nodded, realizing the importance of this perspective. "You're right, Sarah. We often get caught up in the excitement of the present and forget to think about the future. Having common long-term goals can provide direction and purpose to the relationship."

Section 4: Emotional Health and Compatibility

As Sarah and Mark's conversation continued, they touched upon the significance of emotional health and compatibility. Sarah spoke from her own experience, "Mark, it's crucial to prioritize emotional health and compatibility. We need to be with someone who brings out the best in us and supports our growth as individuals. Emotional compatibility ensures a harmonious and loving relationship."

Mark added, "That's so true, Sarah. We should feel comfortable and safe with our partner, able to communicate openly and honestly. Emotional health is the foundation for a strong and lasting connection."

In this chapter, we've explored the foundational principles of setting priorities in dating deliberately. As Christians, our faith is central, but we must also define our values, consider our long-term goals, and prioritize emotional health and compatibility. When we set the right priorities, we lay the groundwork for healthy, God-honoring relationships.

In the next chapter, we'll delve into the practical aspects of dating deliberately, from finding potential partners to navigating the early stages of a relationship. We'll provide you with actionable advice on how to put these priorities into practice and make purposeful choices in your dating journey.

3

Finding the Right Partner

In the cozy corner of a local bookstore, Sarah and Mark continued their exploration of dating deliberately. Having established the importance of setting priorities, they knew the next step was finding the right partner—someone who shared their faith and values. In this chapter, we will delve into the practical aspects of finding a partner who aligns with your priorities as a Christian.

Section 1: Where to Begin

Mark opened the conversation by asking, "Sarah, how do we even begin to find a partner who shares our faith and values? It often feels like looking for a needle in a haystack."

Sarah smiled reassuringly. "It may seem daunting, but remember, God has a plan for each of us. Start by seeking potential partners within your faith community—church, Bible study groups, or Christian events. These environments are more likely to connect you with people who share your beliefs."

Section 2: Online Dating with Purpose

As they sipped their coffee, Mark brought up the topic of online dating. "Sarah, I've considered trying online dating, but I worry about the superficial nature of it. How can we use online platforms purposefully?"

Sarah nodded, understanding Mark's concerns. "Online dating can be a useful tool if used with purpose. Choose platforms that cater to Christian singles, and be clear about your faith and values in your profile. Be patient and take the time to get to know someone before meeting in person. And remember, while online dating can help you connect, it's essential to continue building your relationship in real life."

Section 3: Assessing Compatibility

The conversation shifted to the importance of assessing compatibility. Mark asked, "How do we know if someone is truly compatible with us?"

Sarah replied, "Compatibility goes beyond shared faith; it includes values, life goals, communication styles, and even your spiritual connection. Ask meaningful questions, and don't shy away from discussing your faith and values openly. Assess whether your goals and values align, and if you can envision a future together based on these shared priorities."

Section 4: Red Flags and Deal-Breakers

Sarah and Mark also discussed red flags and deal-breakers. Mark wondered, "What are some warning signs we should be aware of when looking for a partner?"

Sarah advised, "Pay attention to any actions or behaviors that go against your core values or faith. If your partner shows a lack of respect for your beliefs or tries to compromise your faith, it's a significant red flag. Don't ignore these signs; trust your instincts and prioritize your faith above all else."

Section 5: Seek Guidance and Pray

Sarah emphasized the importance of seeking guidance from trusted mentors and friends, as well as prayer. "Mark, we should never underestimate the power of seeking God's guidance in our search for a partner. Consult with wise, godly individuals in your life, and let them provide you with insights and advice. And, of course, pray for wisdom and discernment. God knows the desires of your heart and will guide you toward the right person."

In this chapter, we've explored the practical steps in finding the right partner as a Christian. Start by looking within your faith community, consider online dating with purpose, assess compatibility based on shared faith and values, be aware of red flags and deal-breakers, and seek guidance from trusted individuals while praying for divine guidance.

In the following chapter, we will focus on the early stages of a relationship, including the importance of communication, setting boundaries, and nurturing a strong, God-honoring connection with your partner.

4

Nurturing a Purposeful Connection

In the soft glow of a candle-lit restaurant, Sarah and Mark continued their discussion on dating deliberately, having successfully navigated the challenges of finding the right partner who shared their faith and values. Now, they turned their attention to the critical phase of nurturing a purposeful connection in a romantic relationship. This chapter explores the key elements of fostering a strong, God-honoring bond.

Section 1: Open and Honest Communication

"Communication is the cornerstone of any successful relationship," Sarah began. "It's even more crucial in a God-centered relationship. Open and honest communication not only helps you understand each other's thoughts, feelings, and concerns but also deepens your emotional connection. Share your joys, fears, and dreams, and encourage your partner to do the same."

Mark added, "And, most importantly, listen actively. Show empathy and understanding when your partner opens up. Communication is a two-way street, and it's essential to be supportive and non-judgmental."

Section 2: Setting Healthy Boundaries

Mark was curious about the concept of boundaries. "How do we set healthy boundaries in our relationship, Sarah? And why are they important?"

Sarah replied, "Boundaries are a way to protect and nurture your relationship. They're a sign of respect for each other's individuality and a means to uphold your shared values. Setting boundaries helps avoid situations that could compromise your faith or values. It's a way to keep your relationship God-centered."

Mark nodded in agreement. "So, it's not about restricting the relationship but ensuring it stays in alignment with our faith and values."

Section 3: Quality Time Together

Nurturing a purposeful connection also involves spending quality time together. Sarah said, "Dedicating quality time to your partner is an investment in your relationship. It allows you to create cherished memories, share experiences, and grow closer together. It's a way to strengthen your emotional bond."

Mark asked, "But what if we're both busy with our own lives? How can we find the time?"

Sarah suggested, "It's all about balance. While it's essential to have time for personal growth and commitments, making an effort to prioritize your partner in your schedule shows them that they are a significant part of your life. Even small, intentional moments can make a difference."

Section 4: Praying Together

"Prayer is a powerful tool to maintain a strong, God-honoring connection," Mark mused. "How can we incorporate it into our relationship?"

Sarah smiled. "Praying together is a beautiful way to deepen your spiritual connection. You can pray for your relationship, for each other's well-being, and for God's guidance. It's a means to invite God into your relationship, seeking His wisdom and blessings. Plus, it's a reminder that your faith is at the heart of your connection."

Section 5: Honoring God in Your Relationship

As their dinner came to a close, Sarah concluded, "Ultimately, the goal of a purposeful relationship is to honor God in all that you do. Seek His guidance in your relationship, keep your faith at the forefront, and remember that your commitment to each other is a reflection of your commitment to God."

Mark nodded, feeling inspired by the conversation. "Our relationship can be a source of joy and fulfillment, while also being a testimony to our faith."

In this chapter, we've explored the essential elements of nurturing a purposeful connection in a God-centered relationship. Open and honest communication, setting healthy boundaries, spending quality time together, praying together, and honoring God in your relationship are the keys to building a strong, God-honoring bond with your partner.

In the next chapter, we'll delve into the challenges that can arise in a Christian relationship and how to navigate them while staying true to your faith and values.

5

Navigating Challenges with Faith and Resilience

As Sarah and Mark continued their exploration of dating deliberately, they understood that relationships were not without their challenges. In this chapter, they delved into the obstacles that could arise in a Christian relationship and how to navigate them with faith and resilience.

Section 1: Dealing with Differences

Mark started the conversation by sharing a concern: "Sarah, I've noticed that, even with shared faith and values, differences can arise in a relationship. How do we handle these disagreements without compromising our faith?"

Sarah replied, "Differences are inevitable, but they don't have to be divisive. Approach these situations with humility and a spirit of compromise. Remember that your faith is your anchor, and you can seek guidance from the Bible and prayer to find common ground. It's also a chance to grow in understanding and respect for each other."

Section 2: Outside Influences

"Sometimes, external influences can put pressure on our relationship," Mark noted. "How do we protect our relationship from negative influences or well-meaning but misguided advice?"

Sarah agreed that outside influences could be challenging. "It's essential to establish strong boundaries to protect your relationship from negative influences. Surround yourselves with a supportive community of friends and mentors who share your values and can provide guidance. When receiving advice, be discerning and filter it through the lens of your faith and your unique relationship."

Section 3: Staying True to Your Values

As the conversation continued, Mark brought up an issue that many Christians face: "Sarah, how can we ensure that we stay true to our values and faith, even in the face of societal pressures or temptations?"

Sarah responded, "Staying true to your values and faith requires a steadfast commitment. Remind yourselves why your faith is so important and why you chose to be together. Continually nurture your relationship through prayer, Bible study, and spiritual practices. And when faced with temptations or societal pressures, lean on your shared faith to make decisions that honor God."

Section 4: Forgiveness and Reconciliation

Sarah shifted the conversation to a topic that was vital in any relationship: forgiveness. "Mark, conflicts are inevitable in any relationship. How can we approach forgiveness and reconciliation with our Christian values in mind?"

Mark said, "Forgiveness can be difficult, but it's a central teaching in our faith. We should forgive as God has forgiven us. Seek to understand each other's perspectives, apologize when necessary, and work towards reconciliation.

Remember that forgiveness is a choice, and it can strengthen your relationship by fostering grace and humility."

Section 5: The Role of Prayer and Faith

"Throughout all these challenges," Mark mused, "how can prayer and faith be our guiding lights?"

Sarah smiled. "Prayer is your direct line to God, and your faith is the foundation of your relationship. Lean on these powerful resources for guidance, strength, and wisdom in times of trouble. Your faith can help you see challenges as opportunities for growth, and prayer can bring you closer to God, who can transform your relationship."

In this chapter, Sarah and Mark discussed the challenges that can arise in a Christian relationship and how to navigate them with faith and resilience. Dealing with differences, handling external influences, staying true to your values, practicing forgiveness, and relying on the power of prayer and faith are essential tools in maintaining a strong, purposeful relationship.

In the following chapter, we will explore the beauty of commitment and the significance of a Christian relationship that endures through time.

6

The Beauty of Commitment

In their journey to date deliberately, Sarah and Mark had navigated the challenges, celebrated their shared faith and values, and forged a strong, purposeful connection. As they continued their discussion, they began to explore the beauty of commitment in a Christian relationship. This chapter delves into the importance of commitment, perseverance, and building a lasting, God-honoring bond.

Section 1: The Significance of Commitment

Mark began the conversation by reflecting on the importance of commitment. "Sarah, commitment seems to be the glue that holds a relationship together. What makes it so significant in a Christian relationship?"

Sarah responded, "Commitment is at the heart of a Christian relationship. It signifies the promise to stand by each other's side through thick and thin, in accordance with your faith and values. It's a declaration of your intent to love, support, and nurture the relationship, just as God is committed to us. It's a beautiful and selfless act."

Section 2: Persevering Through Challenges

Mark raised a common concern, "What happens when the initial excitement fades, and challenges start to test our relationship? How do we persevere?"

Sarah acknowledged the reality of such moments. "Challenges are part of any relationship, but commitment allows you to weather those storms. Remember that love is not just a feeling but a choice. Your shared faith and commitment to each other can help you persevere through difficulties. Pray together, seek counsel, and work as a team to overcome obstacles."

Section 3: Building a Strong Foundation

Sarah continued, "A strong relationship requires a solid foundation. How can we continue to build upon the foundation we've established?"

Mark pondered, "Is it about setting long-term goals or continually reinforcing our faith?"

Sarah emphasized both aspects. "It's about setting long-term goals together and ensuring that your faith remains at the forefront of your relationship. Make joint decisions based on your values and aspirations, and regularly revisit your goals to ensure you're both aligned. Your faith should be the guiding light in everything you do as a couple."

Section 4: The Role of Intimacy and Vulnerability

The conversation naturally turned to the topic of intimacy. Mark asked, "What role does intimacy play in a committed relationship? How can we maintain intimacy while staying true to our faith and values?"

Sarah replied, "Intimacy in a Christian relationship is about more than physical affection. It's about emotional, spiritual, and intellectual connection. To maintain this intimacy, continue to be vulnerable with each other. Share your thoughts, dreams, and fears. This deepens your connection and keeps your relationship vibrant."

Section 5: Supporting Each Other's Spiritual Growth

The chapter concluded with a reflection on supporting each other's spiritual growth. Mark inquired, "How can we help each other grow spiritually within the relationship?"

Sarah answered, "Supporting each other's spiritual growth involves encouraging each other in faith practices like prayer, Bible study, and attending church together. Share inspirational materials and engage in spiritual discussions. Your commitment to each other should include a commitment to helping each other grow spiritually."

In this chapter, we've explored the beauty of commitment in a Christian relationship. Commitment signifies a promise to love, support, and nurture the relationship in accordance with your faith and values. It's a pledge to persevere through challenges, build a strong foundation, maintain intimacy, and support each other's spiritual growth. Commitment is the enduring force that makes a Christian relationship resilient and enduring.

In the final chapter, we will summarize the key takeaways from this guide to dating deliberately as a Christian and encourage you to embrace this journey with faith, purpose, and a heart filled with love.

7

Embracing the Journey with Faith and Purpose

In their thoughtful conversations about dating deliberately, Sarah and Mark had explored the essential principles and practical steps for Christians seeking God-honoring relationships. As they approached the conclusion of their guide, they wanted to emphasize the importance of embracing this journey with faith, purpose, and a heart filled with love.

Section 1: Reflecting on Your Journey

Sarah began by encouraging reflection on the journey so far. "As you've learned about dating deliberately, take a moment to reflect on your personal journey. Consider how you've grown, what you've learned, and how your perspective on relationships has evolved."

Mark added, "Remember that this journey is a process, and growth often comes through challenges and self-discovery. Embrace every moment as an opportunity to learn and draw closer to God."

Section 2: Trusting God's Timing

One of the most significant challenges in dating deliberately was waiting for the right person. Mark asked, "How can we trust God's timing when it feels like we're waiting for the right person forever?"

Sarah responded, "It can be challenging, but remember that God's timing is perfect. Use this time to strengthen your relationship with Him, grow personally, and prepare yourself to be the best partner you can be. Trust that God knows the desires of your heart and has a plan for you."

Section 3: Remaining Grounded in Your Faith

Emphasizing the importance of faith, Mark asked, "How do we ensure our faith remains at the forefront of our relationship, even as we face everyday challenges?"

Sarah offered advice, "Integrate your faith into your daily life as a couple. Start your day with prayer together, share spiritual readings, and discuss your faith journey. Attend church services as a couple and actively engage in faith-based activities. By nurturing your faith together, it becomes an inseparable part of your relationship."

Section 4: Celebrating Each Other's Individuality

"Amid all the shared moments," Mark wondered, "how can we celebrate each other's individuality within the relationship?"

Sarah smiled, "While you grow together, it's essential to celebrate and honor each other's uniqueness. Support each other's personal goals and interests. Recognize that individual growth contributes to the growth of your relationship. Encourage each other's dreams and aspirations."

Section 5: Practicing Gratitude and Love

Mark reflected on the power of love and gratitude. "How can we keep love alive in our relationship, and how can we practice gratitude for each other?"

Sarah shared her thoughts, "Love thrives through consistent acts of kindness, affection, and appreciation. Practice gratitude by acknowledging each other's contributions to the relationship. Express your love regularly through words and actions, and keep the flame of love alive with continual acts of service, compassion, and respect."

Section 6: Encouragement for the Journey Ahead

As they approached the end of their guide, Mark shared words of encouragement, "To all those embarking on this journey of dating deliberately, know that God is with you every step of the way. The principles and guidance in this guide are here to support you, but ultimately, your relationship is a unique, beautiful journey that you and your partner will create together."

Sarah concluded, "Remember that your commitment to dating deliberately as a Christian is a profound testament to your faith. Embrace this journey with an open heart, a steadfast commitment to your values, and a strong reliance on God. Your path may have its challenges, but it's a journey filled with love, growth, and a deeper connection with God and each other."

In this final chapter, Sarah and Mark encouraged those seeking to date deliberately as Christians to embrace the journey with faith, purpose, and a heart filled with love. They reminded readers that this journey is a process, and it's a beautiful opportunity to grow personally, strengthen your faith, and build a lasting, God-honoring relationship.

8

Conclusion - Embracing God's Plan for Love

As Sarah and Mark concluded their insightful guide to dating deliberately as a Christian, they wanted to leave readers with a final chapter that served as a summary of the key takeaways and a call to embrace God's plan for love.

Section 1: A Recap of the Journey

Sarah began by summarizing their journey, "Throughout this guide, we've explored the fundamental principles of dating deliberately as a Christian. We've learned the importance of setting priorities, finding the right partner, nurturing a purposeful connection, navigating challenges, and embracing commitment. Each of these steps is crucial to creating a God-honoring relationship."

Mark added, "We've discussed the significance of faith, values, open communication, setting boundaries, and maintaining intimacy. Our journey has been a holistic exploration of what it means to date with intention, purpose, and love."

CONCLUSION - EMBRACING GOD'S PLAN FOR LOVE

Section 2: A Reminder of God's Presence

Reflecting on their conversations, Sarah reminded readers, "In every step of your journey, remember that God is with you. He knows your heart's desires and is actively shaping your path. Trust in His timing and guidance, and seek His wisdom and strength in every aspect of your relationship."

Mark echoed this sentiment, "Your relationship should be an extension of your faith and your love for God. Let His presence be the guiding force, the foundation, and the source of strength in your relationship."

Section 3: Honoring Your Commitment

The importance of commitment was a theme that ran throughout their discussions. "Commitment is the pillar of a lasting relationship," Sarah said. "It signifies your dedication to loving, supporting, and nurturing each other, even in the face of challenges. It's a declaration of your faith in each other and your shared values."

Mark added, "When challenges arise, your commitment to God and each other will see you through. Lean on your faith, communicate openly, practice forgiveness, and rely on the strength of your love to persevere."

Section 4: Embrace the Journey with Gratitude

"As you continue your journey of dating deliberately," Sarah emphasized, "remember to be grateful for the gift of love and companionship. Cherish every moment, even the difficult ones, as they are opportunities for growth and deeper connection."

Mark concluded, "Embrace your journey with faith, purpose, and a heart filled with love. Your relationship is a unique story written by God. Trust in His plan, and keep your faith at the forefront of your relationship."

Section 5: A Final Blessing

Sarah and Mark concluded their guide with a final blessing: "May your journey of dating deliberately as a Christian be filled with love, grace, and the abiding presence of God. May your relationship be a testament to the beauty of faith, commitment, and love. And may you find joy and fulfillment in the purposeful, God-honoring love that you've chosen to embrace."

In this final chapter, Sarah and Mark left readers with a heartfelt call to embrace God's plan for love, reminding them that faith, commitment, and gratitude are the cornerstones of a purposeful, enduring relationship. They encouraged readers to trust in God's guidance and to continue this journey with open hearts, dedicated to living out their faith in every aspect of their love story.

9

Resources and Recommendations

As Sarah and Mark's guide to dating deliberately as a Christian draws to a close, they wanted to provide readers with a valuable resource chapter. In this final chapter, they offer recommendations for books, websites, and organizations to help you further explore and deepen your understanding of faith-centered relationships.

Section 1: Recommended Reading

Sarah and Mark recognized the importance of reading and learning to strengthen your relationship. They shared some book recommendations to help you on your journey:

- The 5 Love Languages by Gary Chapman: This book explores the concept of love languages, helping you understand how you and your partner give and receive love.

- Boundaries in Dating by Dr. Henry Cloud and Dr. John Townsend: This book offers valuable insights into setting healthy boundaries in your dating relationship.

- The Meaning of Marriage by Timothy Keller: A deep exploration of the spiritual and practical aspects of marriage, this book provides valuable wisdom for dating and building a Christian marriage.

Section 2: Online Resources

In the digital age, online resources are abundant and can provide ongoing support and advice. Sarah and Mark suggested the following websites and online communities:

- Focus on the Family (www.focusonthefamily.com): This website offers a wealth of articles, podcasts, and resources on marriage, dating, and relationships from a Christian perspective.

- Boundless (www.boundless.org): A community for young adults seeking a Christian approach to dating, relationships, and marriage.

- The Gospel Coalition (www.thegospelcoalition.org): An online platform with articles and resources on a wide range of topics, including relationships and faith.

Section 3: Seek Guidance and Community

Sarah emphasized the importance of seeking guidance from trusted individuals and being part of a supportive community:

- "Don't hesitate to reach out to mentors, pastors, or other wise individuals within your faith community. They can provide personalized advice and support."

- "Consider joining a local Bible study group or young adults' ministry to connect with like-minded individuals who share your faith and values. Building relationships within your church can provide valuable support on your journey."

RESOURCES AND RECOMMENDATIONS

Section 4: Supportive Organizations

Mark highlighted a few organizations that focus on helping Christians in their dating and relationship journeys:

- Christian Mingle (www.christianmingle.com): A Christian dating site designed to help singles find like-minded partners who share their faith.

- FamilyLife (www.familylife.com): An organization dedicated to helping families and couples build strong, God-honoring relationships. They offer conferences, resources, and articles on relationships and marriage.

- Cru (www.cru.org): Cru is a Christian organization that provides resources, conferences, and community support for young adults seeking to live out their faith in every aspect of life, including relationships.

Section 5: Stay Open to Growth

In their final words of advice, Sarah and Mark encouraged readers to stay open to growth and learning:

- "Remember that your journey in dating deliberately as a Christian is a path of continuous growth and self-discovery. Embrace each challenge and opportunity for learning as a step toward a stronger, faith-centered relationship."

- "Stay rooted in your faith, trust in God's plan, and nurture your love through prayer and worship. Let your faith be the guiding light in your journey."

Section 6: A Blessing for the Road Ahead

As they concluded the chapter, Sarah and Mark offered a final blessing: "May the resources and recommendations provided here help you on your path to dating deliberately as a Christian. May your journey be filled with growth, love, and faith. And may your relationship be a shining example of God's plan for love."

In this resource chapter, Sarah and Mark provided readers with valuable recommendations for books, websites, organizations, and ways to seek guidance and community support. They encouraged readers to continue their journey with an open heart, embracing opportunities for growth and deepening their faith-centered relationships.

10

A Lifelong Journey

In this final chapter, Sarah and Mark reflect on the enduring nature of the journey to date deliberately as a Christian. They emphasize that the lessons and principles they've shared are not just for the early stages of a relationship but for a lifelong journey of love, faith, and commitment.

Section 1: The Ever-Evolving Relationship

Sarah started by acknowledging that the journey doesn't end with a wedding or the initial phases of a relationship. "Dating deliberately is not just about finding the right partner; it's about nurturing your relationship throughout its various stages. Your love will evolve and change, and your faith will continue to be your anchor."

Mark added, "You'll face new challenges as a married couple, as parents, and as you grow older together. The principles of dating deliberately, centered on faith, values, and commitment, will continue to guide you through each stage of your journey."

Section 2: Growing Together in Faith

The discussion turned to the importance of growing together in faith. Sarah shared, "Your faith journey is a lifelong commitment, and it's a journey that you share with your partner. Continue to deepen your faith, explore spiritual practices together, and rely on your shared belief in God as the cornerstone of your relationship."

Mark added, "Studying the Bible, praying together, and attending church services as a couple can help you stay connected to your faith and to each other throughout the years."

Section 3: The Role of Grace and Forgiveness

As relationships endure, Sarah noted that grace and forgiveness play a critical role. "Mistakes will happen, and you'll need to practice grace and forgiveness, not just in the early stages but throughout your journey. Keep in mind that your love is built on grace, just as God's love for us is."

Mark continued, "Remember that forgiveness is not a one-time action but an ongoing process. It's an opportunity to demonstrate God's love in your relationship."

Section 4: Cherishing the Journey

Mark encouraged readers to cherish the journey, stating, "Every moment in your relationship is a gift from God. Even in difficult times, find joy in the journey and in the person you've chosen to spend your life with. Embrace each day with gratitude and love."

Sarah agreed, "Celebrate your love story—your first date, your wedding day, the birth of your children, and all the moments in between. Each step of your journey is an opportunity to deepen your love and faith."

Section 5: A Prayer for the Journey

As a final offering, Sarah and Mark shared a prayer for all those embarking on the lifelong journey of dating deliberately as a Christian:

"Dear God, we pray for all those who have been on this journey with us, seeking to date deliberately as Christians. May your guidance and love continue to light their path. May their relationships be a testament to your grace, faithfulness, and enduring love. Grant them the strength to persevere through challenges and the wisdom to nurture their faith and commitment. Bless their relationships with joy, growth, and an unwavering faith in you. In Jesus' name, we pray. Amen."

Section 6: A Final Blessing

In closing, Sarah and Mark shared a final blessing: "May your journey in dating deliberately as a Christian be a lifelong adventure filled with love, faith, and commitment. May God's grace and wisdom guide you at every step, and may your relationship continue to shine as a beacon of hope, love, and faith to others."

In this final chapter, Sarah and Mark emphasized that the journey to date deliberately as a Christian is not a temporary phase but a lifelong commitment. They encouraged readers to continue to grow in faith, practice grace and forgiveness, cherish every moment, and embrace the journey with gratitude and love. The journey of love and faith is an enduring one, and with God as the foundation, it's a journey that can be filled with joy, purpose, and fulfillment.

11

A Community of Love

In this additional chapter, Sarah and Mark wanted to explore the concept of a community of love, extending the principles of dating deliberately to the broader Christian community. They believed that relationships are not just about individuals but also about how they connect with and contribute to the larger community.

Section 1: The Wider Christian Community

Sarah began by acknowledging the interconnected nature of the Christian community. "When we embark on a journey of dating deliberately as Christians, it's not just a personal endeavor. It's a journey that impacts our larger Christian community. The love and faith we cultivate in our relationships can radiate outward."

Mark added, "Our relationships, whether they are dating relationships or marriages, serve as a testimony to the power of God's love and grace within the Christian community."

Section 2: Supporting and Encouraging Each Other

The discussion turned to the importance of supporting and encouraging one another within the Christian community. "As we navigate the challenges and joys of dating deliberately, we must be there for one another," Sarah noted. "Our faith community can provide valuable guidance and support, helping us maintain our commitment to faith-centered relationships."

Mark added, "Whether we're offering advice to younger individuals who are dating or providing a shoulder to lean on for those experiencing difficulties in their relationships, our collective wisdom and love can be a significant source of strength."

Section 3: Community Involvement

Mark and Sarah also emphasized the role of community involvement in nurturing faith-centered relationships. "Our churches and faith communities can play an essential role in fostering strong relationships. By organizing events, workshops, and gatherings centered on Christian dating and relationships, we can create opportunities for growth and connection," Mark explained.

Sarah agreed, "By participating in these events and engaging with the wider community, we can strengthen our own relationships and inspire others to date deliberately with faith and purpose."

Section 4: Accountability and Prayer

As relationships can be strengthened by accountability and prayer, Sarah and Mark encouraged readers to extend these practices to the wider Christian community. "We should establish accountability partnerships with fellow Christians to support each other in our relationships. These partnerships can help us remain steadfast in our commitment to faith and love," Mark suggested.

Sarah added, "Prayer is a powerful tool. By collectively praying for one another's relationships, we can invite God's guidance and blessings into our love stories."

Section 5: A Testament to God's Love

In their final words on the concept of a community of love, Sarah and Mark shared their conviction: "Our relationships, guided by faith and love, are a testament to God's love within our Christian community. By dating deliberately with faith and purpose, we contribute to the growth and vitality of our faith community as a whole."

Section 6: A Blessing for the Christian Community

To conclude this chapter, they offered a blessing for the Christian community: "May our community be a place where love, faith, and commitment thrive. May we support, encourage, and pray for one another in our journey of dating deliberately as Christians. Together, may we continue to shine as a beacon of God's love, grace, and faith."

In this additional chapter, Sarah and Mark emphasized the concept of a community of love, where the principles of dating deliberately extend to the broader Christian community. They highlighted the importance of supporting and encouraging one another, community involvement, accountability, and prayer as ways to strengthen the Christian community's faith-centered relationships. Ultimately, they saw relationships as a testament to God's love and grace within the larger Christian community.

12

A Continuing Journey

As Sarah and Mark wrapped up their comprehensive guide to dating deliberately as a Christian, they recognized that the journey of faith-centered relationships is a continuing one. This final chapter is a reflection on the path ahead, a reminder of the lasting principles, and a celebration of the enduring nature of love and faith.

Section 1: Reflecting on the Journey So Far

Sarah initiated the conversation by encouraging readers to reflect on their own journey. "Take a moment to look back on your journey of dating deliberately. Consider how you've grown, what you've learned, and how your faith has been a guiding force in your relationship."

Mark chimed in, "Remember that this journey is not just about finding the right partner but about deepening your connection with God and your partner. The principles you've learned are lasting, and they'll continue to serve you well."

Section 2: The Lifelong Pursuit of Faith-Centered Love

The discussion turned to the lifelong pursuit of faith-centered love. Sarah noted, "Your relationship should be a source of joy, purpose, and growth. As you move forward, keep your faith at the forefront, and rely on God's wisdom and love to guide you."

Mark continued, "A faith-centered relationship is not a destination; it's a journey. As you navigate the complexities of life together, know that your faith is a powerful tool for maintaining a strong, enduring relationship."

Section 3: Embracing Growth and Change

Sarah acknowledged the inevitability of growth and change within a relationship. "Your relationship will evolve, and so will you. Embrace the changes, learn from them, and continue to nurture your love and faith."

Mark added, "Your commitment to each other and to your faith will serve as the foundation for adapting to new circumstances and challenges."

Section 4: Encouragement for the Road Ahead

In their final words of encouragement, Sarah and Mark said, "To all those who have journeyed with us through this guide, we encourage you to embrace the road ahead with faith, purpose, and love. Trust in God's plan for your relationship and continue to seek His guidance in all that you do."

Section 5: A Prayer for the Continuing Journey

To conclude the guide, they shared a prayer for those embarking on the continuing journey of dating deliberately as Christians:

"Dear Heavenly Father, we thank you for guiding us through this journey of dating deliberately as Christians. As we continue on this path, we pray for your wisdom, strength, and love to be ever-present in our relationships. May we grow in our faith, love, and commitment with each passing day. Bless our journey, O Lord, and let our relationships be a reflection of your enduring love. In Jesus' name, we pray. Amen."

Section 6: A Final Blessing

In their closing words, Sarah and Mark offered a final blessing: "May your journey of dating deliberately as a Christian be a continuing adventure filled with faith, purpose, and a love that endures. May God's grace and wisdom guide you at every step, and may your relationship continue to shine as a beacon of hope, love, and faith to others."

In this final chapter, Sarah and Mark acknowledged that the journey of dating deliberately as a Christian is a continuing one. They encouraged readers to embrace growth and change, continue their journey with faith, and trust in God's plan for their relationships. The principles they've learned are lasting and will continue to guide them on the path of faith-centered love.

Book Summary: "Dating Deliberately: A Christian's Guide to Relationships"

"Dating Deliberately: A Christian's Guide to Relationships" is a comprehensive and insightful guide that takes you on a journey of faith-centered dating and relationships. Through the wisdom and experiences of Sarah and Mark, the authors, readers gain a deep understanding of what it means to date with intention, purpose, and faith.

The book is structured into twelve chapters, each delving into a specific aspect of dating deliberately as a Christian:

Chapter 1: Setting Priorities
   - Emphasizes the importance of aligning your values and faith with your dating goals.

Chapter 2: Finding the Right Partner

- Provides guidance on discerning a partner who shares your faith and values.

Chapter 3: Nurturing a Purposeful Connection
   - Explores the significance of open communication, trust, and shared aspirations in a relationship.

Chapter 4: Navigating Challenges with Faith and Resilience
   - Addresses obstacles that can arise in Christian relationships and offers strategies for overcoming them.

Chapter 5: The Beauty of Commitment
   - Explores the value of commitment in building a lasting, faith-centered relationship.

Chapter 6: Embracing the Journey with Faith and Purpose
   - Highlights the importance of trust in God's timing and staying committed to your values.

Chapter 7: Embracing the Journey with Faith and Purpose
   - Encourages readers to trust in God's guidance and continue their journey with open hearts.

Chapter 8: Conclusion - Embracing God's Plan for Love
   - Summarizes key takeaways and reinforces the principles of faith, commitment, and gratitude.

Chapter 9: Resources and Recommendations
   - Offers book and website recommendations, as well as guidance on seeking community support.

Chapter 10: A Continuing Journey
   - Reflects on the lifelong nature of faith-centered relationships and the

importance of embracing growth and change.

Chapter 11: A Community of Love
 - Explores the concept of a community of love, where faith-centered relationships contribute to the larger Christian community.

Chapter 12: A Continuing Journey
 - Reminds readers that the journey of dating deliberately is ongoing and encourages them to trust in God's plan.

Throughout the book, the authors emphasize the significance of faith and commitment as foundational elements in a Christian relationship. They stress the importance of open communication, setting boundaries, and maintaining intimacy while navigating challenges with resilience and grace. The book also provides resources for further learning and encourages readers to be a part of a supportive Christian community.

"Dating Deliberately: A Christian's Guide to Relationships" is not only a guide to finding and nurturing love but also a handbook for living out your faith in the context of relationships. It underscores the enduring nature of faith-centered love and encourages readers to embrace their journey with faith, purpose, and a heart filled with love.

www.ingramcontent.com/pod-product-compliance
Lightning Source LLC
LaVergne TN
LVHW010439070526
838199LV00066B/6086